Vortex Street

poems
Page Hill Starzinger

Also by Page Hill Starzinger

Vestigial

Unshelter

Vortex Street

poems
Page Hill Starzinger

Barrow Street Press
New York City

Cover Art: Page Hill Starzinger
Cover Design: Michelle Caraccia
Author Photo: Daniel Dorsa

Published 2020 by Barrow Street, Inc.
(501) (c) 3) corporation. All contributions are tax deductible.
Distributed by:
    Barrow Street Books
    P.O. Box 1558
    Kingston, RI 02881

Barrow Street Books are also distributed by Small Press Distribution,
SPD, 1341 Seventh Street Berkeley, CA 94710-1409, spd@spdbooks.org;
(510) 524-1668, (800) 869-7553 (Toll-free within the US); amazon.com;
Ingram Periodicals Inc., 1240 Heil Quaker Blvd, PO Box 7000,
La Vergne, TN 37086-700 (615) 213-3574; and Armadillo & Co., 7310
S. La Cienega Blvd, Inglewood, CA 90302, (310) 693-6061.

Special thanks to the University of Rhode Island English Department and
especially the PhD Program in English, 60 Upper College Road, Swan
114, Kingston, RI 02881, (401) 874-5931, which provides valuable
in-kind support, including graduate and undergraduate interns.

First Edition

Library of Congress Control Number: 2020930093

ISBN 978-0-9997461-7-2

In memory
of my parents,
Mimi Hill Starzinger (1928–2017)
Vincent Evans Starzinger (1929–2017)

CONTENTS

The earth was an egg, freshened and splitting. . . .

If I swallowed a seed and some soil, could I grow grapes in my mouth?

—*Pilgrim at Tinker's Creek*, Annie Dillard

Else

Go back to the beginning of the beginning and the darkness
                                   filled with 1,000,000 eggs.

Cilia beating their microscopic hairs in the fallopians.

Almond-shaped and pearly grey, ova yolking nucleus to an odor
                        sperm might sense. . . .

    Every month, tumbling out of my body.

                            Something to do with not trusting
myself, this childlessness.
                            Something to do with squandering
        what I'm given.
                            And here
                            one must find gentleness.
The owl of Minerva

                    spreads its wings only with the falling of dusk,
            my father says to me

by way of Hegel, about something else entirely. *We must soldier on.*
                        Send me the bonbons, they'll get me through

to the end.   Who else have
I lost?

I

And: Still

I am a child of
 no one alive,

  no one who
   can remember
      my name.

Fathers,
mothers,
grand,
and great—
they are gone.

My child, will you consider this:

His name was Aylan, three years old.
      Washed up, facedown in a red T-shirt on a Turkish beach.
           On the way to a country that had already
   denied him asylum.

                    *

I was thinking about attention. Not being there.
   And I didn't notice what happened.
         The last two eggs simply
         fell out of myself, tumbling—

                    *

A hospital CEO, rushing to attend a series of meetings
      in Perry, Iowa, *accidentally*
               left her daughter in a minivan in 90-degree heat.

                    *

I hear a baby crying, which he'll never recall.

It's evening and people are still jogging,
                              as if they're running out of time.

My child, will you consider this:

*

I wouldn't hold her.
        Couldn't.
                        Baby girl.
I'd have to give her back.
  She'd
       never be mine.   She'd
  always belong to another.   Why
 feel that.   Cradle until she
 cries and
       give her up?
         Curled in arms, rocked, just to return
her. No:
          I place tips of fingers on her cold toes.
Size of my fingernail they were.
      She didn't seem to notice. Or, maybe, she seemed to   accept it.
   Gazing through me she was. As if I weren't
there. I'm of two minds: the smallest orchid,
       just discovered in a cloud forest:
          unnamed. I almost wish
      we had never found
        it.

*

No child, but I assemble
         the list I would have made:
     Prenatal vitamins
     Folic acid
     Bathroom scale

Fertility monitoring device
Donor egg program
IVF

Asleep, I once dreamt of a blond child—pageboy haircut,
head tilted sideways as if habitual, with me; sea-blue eyes.
Waving at me—he was mine, my boy. Was he waving hello or
good-bye. He never returned. The frame tight,
no
perspective.

*

Does the lotus
really close its petals at night and sink underwater
to rise and open at dawn. On second thought: don't tell.

One could argue the brilliance of Velázquez was that
even his infantas were depicted with profound
individuality,
so lifelike Philip IV supposedly
barked, *What, are you still here?*
Painted in a flash of brushstrokes
—abstract up close, always on the verge
of dissolution.
Now.
And: still—

My Learning Path

Today, my digital learning module says:
　　　　It's crucial that your presence is optimized.
I can see that. My eyes are bleary. I'm baffled and blown over by
　　　　learning how to pull a qualified consumer
　　　　　　　　　　through the purchase
　　　　　　　　　　funnel!

　　　　　　　　Remember
　　Mary Tyler Moore
　　　　　　　　　　tossing her tam-o'-shanter
　　　　up into the city lights   lit sky
　　　　　　　　　　at 7th and Nicollet
　　in a double-breasted peacoat;
　　　　　　that huge smile.　　An unwitting extra,
　　　　just plain old Hazel Frederick,
　　　　　　　　　exits a department store in cat-eye glasses,
　　　　　　　　　　　　　forever caught
　　　　　　　　　　between　　words
　　　　　　in the final credits.

　　　　Today,
The username or password for my *outgoing mail server is*
　　　　　　　　incorrect.　　*I am*
　　　　　　　　　　　bringing content
　　　　　　　　　　　　　　to life,
but there is an issue, I mean　　*opportunity:*
　　　　　　Time Decay.

Shelley Hack
　　　　leaping out of a cream convertible Rolls Royce and
　　　　　　striding into—was it Café Carlyle—
　　　　　　　　　　　　Bobby Short on piano.
　　　First time a woman wore pants
　　　　　　in a fragrance ad.
　　　　　　　　1973.

I must
    abandon the period,
     once a pause,
now, *unnecessarily harsh!* Snap my
   Chat: Thanks
for joining me today as we
  disrupt—.

    Today,
at Celine's runway show in Paris—*the designer who knows*
  what real women want—
   played a soundtrack of far-off city traffic

and children's voices—as if getting dropped off at school.
     Need a trouser suit? A reporter asks.
On every seat
 a quote from artist Dan Graham: *I want to show that our bodies*
     are bound
   to the world, whether we like it
      or not.
Today, I'd say we like it, they are:
   citrus,
     cyclamen, tarragon,
       oak moss
        and
        rose.

   And I will name you, my child.

And you shall exist like a character
    in a
      fictive world so true
  that we touch—
    velvet-petaled starry jasmine

climbing mossy stone walls at the edge
           of a forest
                of unknown parts
                        the wind, catching tendrils,
birds' feathers, dried weeds
           lifting them up in circles. No
                script, no credits, no—

My Unborn Child Says to Me

You are a mouse in a dove's coat.

An apron with hands:
that's what I didn't want to be, I replied.

It's taken you a long time to catch on.

But is it a race?

Time grew tired waiting.

He's sexist.

You're binary.

I don't think I was strategic.

No, you wanted to be free of the past.
                              Untethered.
  To step into a stream like your mother,
          walk one narrow slice
                  of water after another.
                              Mayflies rising.

A world—constantly changing,
                  shimmering.
                      You felt this was New York.

That sounds right.

See, I knew you before you saw the stream.
I lay inside you
          when you curled within your mother.
I was one of your last two eggs—
              you saw me on the sonogram: remember?

I look at my right thumbnail—
misshapen from picking at cuticles. I can't
see this child now,
                    but for the voice.

We come accidentally and try to find our place.

I have been hungry before: in the south of France,
the cypress, the picnics, the boy's lips. Simply too animal.
Unprotected, we were. But everything else receded,
a blaze of heat pushing outward, filling
me. Probably a late period, so I went to his doctor
                    and he recommended a wash,
just from the pharmacie,
                    nothing much.

Yes, I recall: Aix *comes from Latin for* water.
        You
                have never been ready.

I was
pursuing the boy.

*And then you didn't trust
                your body again.*

I think it scared me.

You worry too much about the past.
                        Stop dwelling
there.

Where did you get so bossy? I mean, so
definitive.

I got it from you, dear.

Contraction

Ovating and denticulating and other sundrye sorts: ovary
      at The Top of the flowering Foot-stalk. In the Bottom
of the Calyx. At the Heart of the Fossa: lateral wall of the pelvis:
      follicular, and granulosa, the cortex with stroma. Still
whitish but no longer almond-sized, now shrunken
      to one centimeter, approximately half absorbed. What is
secreted. Do you see that life will become a thing made of holes.
      Maimonides stated the act of creation
comes from nothing, and thus the void moved from sacrilege
      to holiness. I say, *Nature will not name itself* and *light has no
grammar.* Remember Brunelleschi demonstrated the power
      of an infinite zero: a vanishing point—

Physicists Simulate Sending Particles of Light into the Past, Strengthening the Case that Time Travel Is Possible

Oh nameless one.

As yet unnamed.

Though
      left unnamable—

of unconceivable

    colors:
                inwrought with flowers.

        Nomen nescio,

Prenom
        nescio.

        Nescire.
            Walking

       backward

    and forward until

       the flattened turf
catches
     sunlight

      and becomes
             visible
   as a line.

I would teach

        you how to cross over

bunny ears.
        Rabbit running
around a tree.
        Hiding from a dog, jumping in the hole.

—As simple as a track in the snow or a stone circle—

everything I could not. May not. Will not.
        Want.

Specula

To the man pressing the sonogram over my ovary,
        who is saying, *It's completely shut down*:
it is still part of my body
it is alive
it is mine.
        I want to know:
    Is it velvety when you hold it?
    Is it ghostly white?
    Is it fragrant?
    Does it hum?
            This is where all my children
                        would have sprung
                        if you could time-lapse back:
        magnificent glands,
        corrugated, grooved
                    and furrowed:
alea, meaning *dice*
        as in aleatoric music: Mozart
        selected a precise sequence
                of notes
        based on throwing
                    a handful.

                *

        Beauties, we are,
            we say *beautiful*:

        estradiol in our
                        vaginas
                and windswept fires   in our veins.

                *

Oblivion.

Yes, that

        moment. *I can't help thinking*
it must be a little choppy, Philip Larkin said.
    I am going to the inevitable, he squeezed
      his nurse's hand
       right before. Yes,
       1:24 a.m.

    As a fly fisherwoman
        steps into the stream
   on the other side of the world,
wading through water with atoms older
  than the solar system,
    trout eggs buried
      in gravel nests, two eyes develop, and the alevin
hatch, absorbing golden-saffron yolk sacs
  until they can slip free of the stones,
    dark fry swimming up
      into the
          sun.

    *

    Velvety &
     intensely saturated
       in a single   simile, I mean

smile.
    Our lips. Smear of shade named Captive.

    *

           What of need,
         when you want less?

When you think   you want less.
      When the self is   less, you think:
Look how my bones   osteoporosis
         my pelvis   endometriosis,
      my ribs fractious. This is the
         house, my
    house, my only home,   I own   no other.
I lease
      one car.
This is the   my body,
      the beauty—yes—I
           abandoned. To feed
on more expensive
      tastes. A cage to decorate
      became a cage to pain,
this structure, this cage—
if I could build a cage instead. How do you disinherit
your self. Tectonic, indeed.
      Normal faults
         create space
      when the ground cracks,
but as one tectonic plate forces itself
      on another, this is a thrust fault.
I am full of faults.
      Natural
    mistakes, they lie
until uncovered. Fun
       fact:

A fault under the Himalayan peaks
      pushes them up by a centimeter
each year. . . .

  *

    Would my life coach think this was busywork?

  *

I want to hold
all that remains:
iron in our blood,
calcium in our bones,
oxygen we breathe
tracing back to starburst.

And in our DNA

roses and petals fall around us as
sounds of the audience during Philip Glass's composition
without musicians. Not an attempt to bring order out of chaos
but—waking up to the very life we
are living.

*

Ivory, bone—
faces marked

with dots. Who do I think I am?

*

If you think about less
you consider
microbes from the world's oceans
—so tiny until 50 years ago scientists didn't
realize the specks were alive:
now 40 million genes identified
in upper layers of seawater—
constantly dancing, keeping our ecosystem
balanced.
Some
faults
release earthquakes. Others
release
energy, quietly.

*

Doors opening to doors flung wide   imprint of window frames
you see from one end to the other and out to crab apple   unpruned
    past front door with five random locks

*

        as if I weren't going to save anything to pass on.

*

        Her name was Page
                and she let people write stories
all over her
                        her name was Page
                        and she was a   writer, and though she
                            didn't believe it,
I do.
                    Her name was Page and she
was nothing
        but a sheet of paper

            that's the story
            and it's an old story
her name was Page
        and she wrote it down.
                Her name was Page and she was *born of women to live*
                            awhile and fall and die.

        *

Then you go home and forget it.

        *

Her name was Page and the skin on her hands
                                        was becoming invisible.
            You could see blue veins
                    through thinning

20

membrane.
Small spongy discs
        in her spinal column
                                        were
compressing.
    Yet her knee looks wider, not as
    graceful.
                                        Her name is Page
            and she is almost exactly
—and at the same time—not at all what she was.
                        If you only love
                                    what you can't possess,
                    she should love herself   immensely.
If body is reparation,
            she could skin
            all the stories written over her torso
                    and bind
                        them
                        in
                        a book,
                        thin muslin psalm of self.

II

OO

                Likely   it happened in a different way.
                    It's a story
                                    I can rewrite.
                        It's my story,
        I can rewrite it.
                        There are things to see clearly:
                    A. I never went out of my way to have
                                            a child.
                    B. The endometriosis was
                                    severe, I lost an ovary, appendix . . . .

        See
                        I had choices,
                            others took them. Plural.
            People can, and will,   adapt. I
        mean adopt.

        Grief is something to revise. Or,
                    to sit with quietly. Try to
                                sit with quietly.   Even the
                        quietly
            is difficult.   Itchy.

                    C. I am fearful of something going in my body.
                                Afraid of not taking proper care.
                    This is not going well.
                                I'd like to end

                                as soon as possible.
                        Ooplasm
                is the yolk of the ovum.
                                Germinal, nutritive, paired and the ovaries suspended,
                                tethered by ligaments
                                to the peritoneal cavity.
        These are facts one can start with.

Sentence

Holding a mayfly with a 24-hour life span.
Walking on rock 350 million years old.
I almost drove off the bridge in the snowstorm, my father said.
My grandmother's face, my mother's, my own.
      Rentrayage is to remake, reweave: across the cut.

Getting stuck in the middle of the word, the vowels.
My mother ran her hand over her face, surprised.
She didn't remember what it felt like: stubble, flaking skin.
Because you've determined I'm wrong: that's the first trespass.
      It repeats—I must have something to do with it.

Songbird flying headfirst into tinted glass.
Mistaking reflection for habitat.
I'll slip out so quietly no one realizes I've left, including myself.
It's a privilege, inherited: to refuse. Not to wear the fox.
      In what ways are we still pointing our ski tips together?

I Am

apparently lost
  at
       locating

       wherever
they expected I
would go;
I confuse
cardinal directions,
hardwood species, vegetation
zones, blooming
         periods . . .
They rise and vanish in oblivious host.

      Here is   the question—
   my question: can I find the wet moss on granite
   can I find the   scent of mountain
       ferns   damp emerald
luminous in the dark   silvered dusk bird singing
near the worn red barn   while small pines frost-shattered
       gnarled   slant into bedrock
    against hillocks?

     *

Humiliation
    is the Buddha's   first noble truth.

     *

After he was naked

27

and scorned,
Richard III—
buried under monastery, later municipal parking lot—
disappearing   *none cares or knows*
500 years.   *Into the nothingness . . .*
                    Into the living sea of waking dreams.
Roman nail
    lodging slowly
into his curving vertebrae. Grave
                forsaken,

        until now.

Parable

Here is the throat. So small.

                                In southern Siberia, herders
of goats and reindeer sing from deep within their larynx: *Khoomeii*—
                sounds like the wind swirling
among rocks—or a mother camel who's lost
her calf: six pitches oscillating simultaneously
across the wide open steppes of Tuva,
where Turkics, Mongols, and Manchu
ruled.
            Tie a prayer ribbon
to a

cairn. In the cold fog
of grasslands—native to violet-veined iris and phlox—
                        new luxury boom-cities rise, espaliated
with Japanese maple, beds
of roses. No one sleeps here—tens of thousands of houses, and dozens
                of office buildings—a speculative
real estate bubble, a ghost
town. And
                                the cat
still laps yak milk: smooth tip of tongue
            lightly touching surface, pulling upward at high speed,

drawing a column of
liquid
behind it, jaws closing and swallowing. A blur—
invisible has many facets, and disappearing
becomes a legacy. Women were prohibited from singing
so they practiced while milking cows,
lulling children to sleep or drinking
araga. A feeling of
                                scarcity. *Hide* is both vellum
and retreat. In these harmonics, the mouth

does not need to be closed, but it demonstrates the point
                                    better. Tongue rises and

seals around gums—and
air is pushed to the
            tiny hole
behind molars. Lips
forming
     a bell-like
shape.
He that hath hid can find.

Of Liberty

—as if you don't see
                    me:
maybe no
curiosity
to wonder, and especially
to ask, much less
        listen.

            Step 354 times up to the crown.

Andy Inkster, transgender, left his
female reproductive organs
intact, gave birth
to a daughter, Elise,
as a man. *If you have a body part*
that does something
        why not use it?

            Encircling the head—
            seven rays
            of sun, seas and continents.

At an Ivy League college in the north woods—
lone pine its icon—
a blogger posts a "rape guide"
targeting an individual
with photo, name, address, and
tips. Perpetrator? Still
        active student.

            Her halo, at first a *pileus*—Roman cap
            of emancipation.

Ysabel stands on a toilet
just to find air to breathe

at a southern Arizona Detention Center.
Incarcerated without bond
—seven months—
despite a federal judge
granting her asylum.

      Skin? Heated copper sheets
      beaten with wooden hammers.

The Russian band Pussy Riot
staged a "punk prayer":
anti-Putin, anti-misogyny.
Jailed 21 months. "Feminism
is perceived as something
dangerous . . . and senseless,"
says Anonymous.

      Broken shackle and chain
      half hidden by robes: symbols
      of abolition deemed
      too divisive after the Civil War.

—Later to be tied
           or held down
at the wrists:
      it felt oddly, deeply familiar,
some safe house of
         captivity—heart, and
      mind. Until I

     figured out   why.

Hook

To
    hang
        from heels,
            24 articulating
        vertebrae
    falling
into their own

curves, this
    backbone—
        same
            for swans
        as sloths.
    Dangling
thread

of *bored young men*
and *beautiful deer*, they called her,
who *vanished*,
did not respond
for article
headlined *Gang Rape, Routine and Invisible*.
Is one surprised. Now
reporting:
Huh is the only
universal
human word, not
mama, as linguists believed. Especially
as Carmen Tarleton emerges
with a new face stitched to her scalp
after her husband beat her with a baseball bat,
soaked her with industrial lye squirted from a dish-soap bottle.
A spinous process, downward and backward
to the sacral
pelvic girdle.

Atlas and axis aligning, like a
bow spring—

Black Apples

Dropping to the red earth, these, the night-bearing
    difficulties of the
21st century orchard. Thrashers calling family
  from spindly
fruit tree-tops, reminding me of the usefulness of dead
  branches. Orange haze over town.
              Lights mingling with planets,
                planes, and stars. Micrometeorites
  raining down more or less continuously
without melting.
     My father thinks I'm his wife
and my mother
     has no idea who I am: at least she asks.
Oh, she responds when I say, *You have a daughter and a son.*
  Not sure she knows what those are anymore.
        Haloperidol
  is prescribed for his agitation—
    look it up: also for alcohol withdrawal. Jeez,
      if only we'd known
        long ago, though he never would have taken it.
  But what
if we hadn't—done what he wanted—always. Nothing
    more than bits on fire,
but they were us. This year
       a new cloud was recognized:
apocalyptic waves, as if a roughened sea seen from underneath:
       Asperitas for short.
  Because no one hangs around for long.

III

Excavations from the Tomb of the Second Pharaoh, 12th Dynasty

No, thanks
       I don't want to take the survey.
Patti Smith buried blue glass beads
                          in an urn next to the headstone. Grave
                          indeed.
           Do you deny yourself what you most want.
      If you don't interrupt   we can have a conversation.
What happened to self serve.
                  Self-serving bias.

I just don't remember.

The young waxer touches me in a way I know she thinks I'm old.
        I recognize it because I
                       touch my mother this way. This
is me. Stripped bare. A knee I don't know. A long back
that's familiar. A stranger's breast.   How
do you settle
          in a body for so long,
                still want it to change. Still
it changes. Annotated legs, enlarged knuckles, skin tone muddied,
      some firm padding
  gone.   I ask the guard

                        where Middle Kingdom is
          and he shows me.
Coffins with mummies tipped sideways, heads lined up
                       with blue-rimmed eyes
       so they can see life
          through the casket.
                  Leg, lotus,
                      snails, snakes,
         ankh.
       Necklaces, so delicate,

amulets strung on thin
strings, lack of clasps. And they survive.

Habituate

It isn't the answers you give.
   It's questions you
don't ask.
     As if responses
         would—of course—
               need overlooking.

Everywhere I consider exits and doorways,
    potential places to hide
           and things to
barricade.

Cleaning out the barn
   you kept a doll,
      though I'd forgotten it. Don't
speak for me.

I won't need much,
     Mother says.
       Her marionettes come to mind.
        Papier-mâché,
shredded newspaper
          soaked in glue—
   as if holding it together
       were this easy.
And not beautiful.
      Thus, multiple baggies of smudge-resistant mascara,
      waterproof eye
      primer.
Nevron, the root
      of puppet, means *sinew,*
muscle   *strings:* and you
don't even know

     how to pull them.

Sidewinder

You say I rudely cut her off, that you had to apologize,
and yet you know nothing—I
looked her in the eye,
she didn't move, speak; I
waited, still nothing—
it seemed as if she was waiting for someone, a husband?—
I have given up waiting, I'd like you to know.

I was near to invisible.

I have almost cut my tongue off.

May I say: I don't want to be entered anymore. I have no use
for it. No pleasure.

Staying in the motel on the exit ramp,
cars back and forward all day, night.
Just watching, sometimes. A little more hunched. And then
a white rabbit between the road and our building.
So dirty.

The Weather Channel says an avalanche starts with two small grains.

I am planning to give everyone a microphone so they can hear the
                                             invisibles.
They may be shy, sick of, happy with, the silence.

How can I tell you what you need to know?

Burrowed in sand, small,
with a rattle. Lethal
to little creatures. Dangerous to people:
hemotoxic venom, they call it. Permanent
damage, it demands medical
attention. The experts say: Leave it
alone.

XX

Told to be self-aware,
     Nice. What comes to mind
          is *flaw*—
700 years old, it first meant flake
        of snow, spark
             of fire, fragment
     gone astray.
On Facebook, men say it's ok
              to use our father's name
    but not our mother's—*no way,*
        it brings us ridicule and embarrassment—
and gradually over time her name is forgotten:
     only mother of the oldest son.
    Flake from some Low German fishing net.
Wattled hurdle.   Frame or
        rack.
And ethicists want to set up inherent limits
        on how much humankind
    should alter nature.
           So we scramble after
        Canada snow geese
      during molting to harvest
  fallen feathers for
          harpsichord quills.
Drifting through Earth's atmosphere
    scattering light
        through imperfections:
    small crystal facets
     supercooled,
     complex,
    no two (isn't that nice) the same.

Vortex Street

I tied my hands behind me so I won't hurt you,
but they get loose: slicing, etching the language of a strange
heart into sweet skin. You love the holly—knife-sharp
leaves, bloody berries trickling ink-stains. Looks like
Christmas, or an olde faerytale.
Will you save me?
Or tell me again
about the mud-dauber nest
like a pan flute, laying eggs in a pipe;
and when it's tuned, larvae break out.
Catch me if you can. Then repeat: as
mother. *How would you*
raise your child differently?
mine asked. How
indeed. I'd like to reference
the laws of probability,
but all that comes to mind
is the mud dauber is unlikely to sting,
unlikelier to sing.
Or is it that we just can't
hear it?

Breaking Wheel

And so we believed:

     Hanging

cathedrals down from heaven,
  blind pierced traceries—
      circular,
          compartmentalized
             stained
     oculi,

  looks like a rose,
    named for the saint
             we sentenced to execution
       on a spiked
     wheel:
Catherine.

      Bones of collars,
forehands
          and toes, spurred
magnificence,
      splayed with lavender veins
         like lacework:

    I
tear apart the prayer-bead pods,
spilling scarlet
     poison over
   the thin luminous place where
mothers hand us their

     habits.
Not only because of the girl
    who lost her sight

carving 100 ivory elephants
to slip into
red

rosary pea-seeds.
Or the mother hawk's
breaking femur
as metal wildlife bands
and fishing wire
constrict her leg.

Or the daughters in a small town
awakening
from naps—stuttering, twitching,
arms flailing, uttering
strange sounds: *hysterical
epidemic.*

It's
no longer to have to follow the father.
To see
the mother falling, splintering
our looking glass.
For her to fall again.

To lift her up. For her to let me.

The Last Day We Were All Together

I'm reminded of being cradled
      in the hull of a boat,
hearing the crackling of
      pistol shrimp
—one claw of millions of creatures
      closing at lightning speed, again
and again.

*

Of a wash, a wadi or an arroyo:
      dry riverbeds cleansed of any sense
of plainness or constancy, collecting in their furrows
      dry leaves, trellised twigs flung up
in high reaches of trees. A fullness achieved
      not in spite of volatility
but out of it.

*

I gave hospice a list for my mother:

1. napkins to fold
2. yarn to wind into a skein
3. art books to look through, especially *Paul Klee: Hand Puppets* with 50 papier-mâché creatures created for the artist's son, Felix—out of scraps of cloth, found objects; *The Cut-Outs*—Henri Matisse replaced paints with scissors during his last decade when confined to his bed, making collages that evoked places he could no longer visit
4. poetry of nature, night, and animals

*

Psithurism:

Of walking through a family of white pines
        as the wind stirs—
trunks and millions
        of needles, each slightly different
from the other: singing a restless lost understory. Listen
        now . . . *lysten*—

        *

List hospice handed me:

    1.   lip swabs for gums and teeth to replace toothbrush
    2.   shampoo caps since she can't shower any longer
    3.   dry mouthwash

        *

First they said 24 to 48 hours;
next, days to weeks.
Her heart rate 35: *unsustainable*—
        waking up with a smile, she is.
She might pass away with little warning
        or sleep more and more until she just doesn't wake up.

        Could she find the hard ground instead of floating
        unmoored.

        *

Tongue furrowed
    with dehydration,
        she says, *I want this to end.*
My father is ripping up his books.
    First Ascent of Mont Blanc: A True Story by T. Louis Oxley, 1881
is one I recover. He throws out
    detailed lists of his climbs, 1949–1951, 1981–1983:
        Zermatt, Courmayeur. . . .

*

Hearing goes last,
   but my father has mostly lost his already. He says *K2* over and over—
because it's as challenging as dying? Because many don't survive?
       So quickly we come around to an end
                                  we can't talk our way through,
           two souls, friends
       since 6th grade, married
   at 24. We look at their bridal photos;

     *

   hardly recognize the faces.
My father mistakes
       me for his
wife. *Are you strong?* he wonders—
before showing me the album,
wedding on the terrace porch, full-out martooni reception on
        the gently rolling lawn—.

     *

Who are we, where do we come from, where do we go.
How can we leave each other.
How could we stay together.
So many questions,
arranging and rearranging,
like our atoms.

Wild carrot, white clover,

     *

strange orange and purple sunset skies,
can anyone promise
that I will still see them at the end. Will you take me out so I can
feel the air lifting up from the river

blowing through white pine and pitch,
over meadows and up into the house we grew up in,
yellow clapboard, mice,

      *

orchids and poems, encyclopedias and sailboats,
barn cats. Time plays quite a trick on us,
drains out so fast, no sound.

Please bury me with nothing but

air and light,   mix in white jasmine

blow a kiss into   my ashy cloud

as it floats, falls,

      *

disintegrates. Earth and   jimson weed,

            third crop of dandelions.

IV

Vocal Balance

Did you know the earth hums?—
as in a vibratory body responding
in harmonic likeness. Perhaps
because it expands and contracts slightly
all the time, or perhaps it's—just—the slap of ocean waves.
We don't know
yet. Above me,
the sound of feet pacing
on the ceiling—grey and sooty, overcast:
as if the inhabitant likes to swing a pendulum and has a plan.
Facing the mirror in front of me, seeing not myself but my
mother, a cellular song braiding and unwinding
around a moment, this and many others.
Ensorcelling—as much about
arrival, as anything else. As in
Old Occitan *arribar* (11th cent.),
language
of troubadours.   E'sôrsəl.
When John Cage visited
an anechoic chamber, he expected silence but heard two sounds,
one high—his nervous system—and one low—
his blood circulation. We are ambient, though:
my spinal discs
cantilevered, irregularly. I
read that mountains are shaped as much by erosion—
raindrops, even—as by
tectonic plates. It is most certainly the end of something.
Tell me, my
matrilineal mitochondrial DNA: what
are the stories embedded there? Is there a way
to hear what's coming?—even
the clef: the pitch
of the stave.

About a House

This is a poem about a house.
Scratch that. This is about
a family. It might be yours.
    Mother and father in matched single beds.
    Siamese sprawled on the floor,
            her kidneys giving out giving

                                    out.

                        *

                    When we sold the house,
        my father left the ice axe nailed to his study door: a handle,
                    long rusted snout hanging
            down. Found on Mont Blanc.
                How will I die: grasping the ice axe,
                    belay of strange falls.
            How these things
                        scatter. A European climber's
ice axe attached to the door of a professor's study in a little yellow
            clapboard house in a Vermont village.
            The daughter wants it back.
                    How many other people know
                        44 Elm Street has a dead climber's
                    axe from the Alps
                            as a door opener?
                What will become of
            the ice axe? Thrown like rubbish
            into a landfill, just
                compacted waste density.
                        Opening nothing.   Closing nothing.
            Neither held nor looped. Worn
                leather leash.
                    On the front door my father attached
            a metal grip from his rowing shell.
                    Secondhand, the boat was his second,

and he named it the same as his first,
               which was called when he bought it
                              από κανέναν, Greek for "from no one."
          Back and forth, he rowed
     the Connecticut River 20 miles a day,

     59,600 miles in his lifetime,
     free of dams
     for 30 miles. All without knowing how to swim.
     You see, you can hang on
                              to wooden shells, they float,
     and someone will come save you.
This is his story;
     his story is a family.
          He was a political-science teacher
who liked
     history.
  Handhold. Toehold.
          Google Street View
     will update and archive 44 Elm. How long? If
the house is torn down, will old photos still
               be stored.
          How much can be saved.
          In this town of Norwich,
          after Norwich, Connecticut,
     spelled Norwhich in the charter,
pronounced Norritch at first
               (like the English).
          Once home of the Abenaki,
               part of the Dawn Land.
               And what of the ways the wild deer and moose
                    call to it?

               *

     I said, *I wish we could keep the house, not to live in,*
     but to visit. No, my father said, *don't do that, it's not a good*

house. The basement isn't even a full basement. Rooms shelved
with books, onionskin-paper encyclopedias: you
could see through words, rippling as they turned. Too
scared of tearing, I left them alone. Gold-embossed
novels, too dense. My father always seemed

        sensible.

       *

    I planted annuals—
    pansies, sweet peas, I don't know what else;
    flowering things you can change with the season, you thrust
        your hands in the soil in spring and in fall;
            countlessly the dirt rearranging itself,
                respirating, filtering. . . .

       *

    A student remembers my father explaining natural law:

In *The African Queen*, Humphrey Bogart wakes up in the boat to see
Katharine Hepburn dumping his gin into the river and he's very upset.
It's only natural, ma'am, that a man should want to drink every now and then.
That's one view of natural law. Hepburn says, *Nature, Mr Allnut,
is what we are here to rise above.* That's the other view.

       *

        I planted two baby fir trees
      at the east and west corners
        at the edge
          of a bank tumbling to meadow,
           Blood Brook rising to hills marked
      by white-tailed deer and black bear.
      Northward, the wind rustling and singing—
      broken   choral   fugue.

*

         About the route
over the Alps Hannibal took
to conquer Rome,
my father says,
Do you remember when
   your mother and I were trying to find it?
I'm reading all the books again.
All 21.   Eighty-seven and has nowhere
to go. The doctors just took away his
car.

         *

What does he think when my mother calls him daddy.
When she thinks I'm his wife.

When she thinks their son is her husband.
Or when he says he'll never

take an airplane again
or go to Iceland

or carry a wreath to the abandoned cemetery in the woods.

When he closed the office, he said good-bye
                                        to the seamstress next door.

You could go back, I said. *I never go back,* he said.

Once a moose loped down the driveway—all we saw were long legs,
his head so high. Did he go into the neighbor's yard. Where
                                        did he go.

My father said:
Lots of people go to the symphony, they do things. We're hermits.

He contracted a boat builder to panel my brother's bedroom. And, eventually my brother lived on a sailboat for 12 years.

My father's right eye is overflowing. His left hip is convulsed. He marked the graves of the cats with fake flowers on sticks. He knows exactly which bloom goes with Petra, Mischievous, Venus and Curious. . . .The new owner has taken the blossoms away. Hacked out old Dutchman's pipe (home to swallowtail butterfly), tangle of honeysuckle, low lilacs leaning over brush. She's put up a tall deer fence.

*

Lying in a grassy hollow on Blood Hill,
my body covered in granite:
as I breathe, rocks rise and fall,
rolling off. Lungs
like a pair of anvils: repeating:
  until almost free of weight—
        gestatus.   Then,
I lay for a long time because I know
I probably can get up.

*

He rustles around in a drawer. He shows me a clock that's broken.
In his pocket, there's a watch that works.
Something about keeping track of time, I guess. Or
  how difficult it is to keep the machinery in order. Or did he want
    me to take the clock in.
        Or was he just showing me things.

*

Is there anything I can do for you? I ask.
There's nothing I need,
he says, *just time.*

60

*

I guess this is a poem about

growing.

I saw a small-scale vintage ladder-back chair in the barn.
My brother said my father had bought it for my children,
which I never had.

My brother said, *You should have it.* I thought about it
overnight. Could I live in my apartment with the chair, empty,
without a child. No little baby. None. Not missing. Never there.
Not. None. From the Middle French for the ninth hour
(early 12th cent) i.e. 3 p.m. and its etymon classical Latin *nona*
(see NOON n): when time breaks you can feel it in your body at
noon when half the day is done and again at 3 p.m, when you
are going home. When time shifts something is over and cannot
be brought back anymore. Irreparable. I decided I would have
the child because I would have the chair. The chair was the child.
I told my father I would like the chair but he said, *Oh no, you don't
want this chair,* he looked away. I said, *Oh yes, I'd like this chair.* He
didn't look at me. He auctioned, with other furniture, the chair.

*

Caning is a flowering.
No caning is not a flowering.

No flowering is a caning.
No, no, caning is nothing of

A flowering. Nothing of. Not.
Nor a. No nother. Notherwise.

No noderways. Not Cane. Flow-
er is not. And Able. None o-

Other than mother. As for moth-
er caning. Nothir of her. Sit-

ting on the cane. Nodur.

*

Mildred. Millie. Mimi. My mother.

The sun came up in the east—
this was her room, our room to share,
the door ajar
                            to let the cats roam free.   One day a raccoon
                            ambles in
and rushes out. She

              inks woodblock prints, writes poetry,
                    ties flies, needlepoints.

The living room was a bloom
                                of orchids,
              shaded,
              cool air sifting through warped wood
              sashes. Whirling sepals,
              medial petals
              and adnate filaments. Shades of celadon,
              fuchsia, cream. Scent of
              honey. Chocolate?

I thought it was all in our veins
until I remembered Louise's greenhouse.
Louise ran my grandmother's house—
that's one way to put it—and left my mother with something
              that became part of us.
              Will I leave a part of myself
                    with others even if
              I have no children.
              How
              flowers connected us backward.
              Mom and I chose huge blooming summer blossoms
              for chairs, blue-of-the-sky for the bedroom floor.

*

Mother doesn't want dates on the cemetery stone.
So you can't tell when she was here and not.
But she didn't ask us to delete her name.
Thrown in the river, her ashes, is what she wants.
Remember how she would hold the fish, feel them,
catch and run. Part of the seep of water and rocks.
It flows over us.
It flows between us. . . . Not just a swerving, but a throwing back,
As if regret were in it and were

sacred.
I'd like to carry her home,
as if she is some other part of me—
lost, broken. Bent double,
she holds her palm up to mine.

How many times did she leave the house
trying to walk home.

*

Weep-drop is based on an erroneous reading of *wete droppes*
in 1876.   *To weep (a thing) back: to*
recover . . . extinguish

*

A reporter wrote on July 2010 of *a silver-haired woman*
walking over the bridge between Norwich and Hanover weekday mornings:
her posture, her profile, symmetry of her perfectly wrapped
hair bun
on the nape of her neck. . . . I feel like she's an old friend
even though I've never said a word to her.
They told the time of day by her, she walked
and walked in circles around the town, the house, the rooms. Now,

pivoting
out of her black chariot.
    Unraveled white strands

      scatter in the wind

        *

      I return after the furniture is gone
      to see 44 Elm one last time:

doors opening to doors flung wide

      imprint of rugs on worn oak floors

    curve of chair against white walls

      outline of couches & picture frames

      row on row of bookshelves,

emptied. All of the bird nests, feathers, rocks and small things

on the mantelpiece, gone. Five random locks,

      I unfurl them, open up the front door,

   and go to the side porches,

      opening everything that's not painted shut.

Edge Effect

Invertebrate now, soft parts but eroded inner disarticulation of muscles
    and a girdle; we hold on to the oddest things. And they to us:
smattering of barnacles and brachiopods attached to calcareous outer
    covering caught in drift along strandlines. Coquinas. Or "butterfly
wings," we called them. Every summer we'd watch them squirm
    into sugary, quartz-crystal sand, weathered and washed from
Paleozoic Blue Ridges. I can't tell these days if my mother is just
    acting, as if she remembers her self. Or me. But still asks, *Can
I help you?* Small saltwater clams, agile, with pointed sharp-edge
    foot, align into earth-crust, migrating vertically and horizontally, able
to dig back in, leap and ride currents, like others extending siphons to the
    surface, water drawn in and expelled: clarifier, stirring suspension.
I'd like to go home. She insists. *How long are we staying in the
    hotel?* Incontinent, a shell of shadows—and shallows: we're at the
edge itself, where increased erosion from groins and tidal walls is
    disrupting flow and sensitive dwellings. Prey: regurgitates grit of
chitinous matter, leaving gobbets of inedible remnants. Rough coffin.
    One wishes for grace. Finds sediment.

Complicit

There's the village my friend calls
un lieu-dit or *also called place,*
a village without administration.
Think how Hamas blew a hole
in the wall dividing
Egypt from Gaza, so donkeys and bicycles
could finally cart back bags of flour, cases of Coca-Cola,
chocolate and antacid. This is an opening,
love. It calls for defiance, and every
last stubborn cell of yours
is up for the fight—that's what I think. And you?
I know you like the teakettle just so
on the burner. Here, look: Ala Shawa
and his wife, Hana, walking through the dirt
into Egypt, her hair fashionably streaked.
Adel al-Mighraky, smoking a Malimbo,
We were like birds in a cage. This is giddiness,
and mayhem. Don't think about it too hard.
And please don't seal the breach.

V

Age

Waking up at 3 a.m. thinking my mother is trying   to
reach me, is she ready to go *now*—or is she lost—
is she lonely—is she hell-
bent on the next—and what if.
Is she the voice of the sharp birds, *here?*
Of the waves on the rocks, *there?*
Is she hitching a ride on the long strings of sargassum floating past?
Is she drifting in clouds of Saharan dust?
Mother,
where is your
black chariot—
iguanas perched on its high back,
dewlap and spiky spines, third eye guarding,
bananaquits circling   like wreaths of smoke,
white gardenias
tied at armrests:

you will clap and smile, your green eyes.
Your duffle always packed at the end of your bed.

*

Route 113 Bridge:
that's the name.
That's the one.
My brother and I will drop you—
ashes and wedding ring—deep
into the river, you, nestled in a rock-salt urn
destined to sink immediately, bio-
degrade.   You wanted brown paper and a rock, but
impact would fling you into the wind
and that's   not what you wanted.

*

Last night
wings beating against the top of the door
ill-fitting in its frame
wrong, the draftsmanship or the craftsmanship, the sawing—

*

Where does grief go
  when it can't escape.

*

Even yesterday, David sprains his ankle
     for the sixth time,
     only 62,
     now, shuffling with a cane:
A-G-E, spells the doctor, as if there were a child in the room.

Barnacles, I say.

Even the beetle on the floor, upside down, when we come home
to our rented house, after driving down the road with the sign—
Caution: Watch out for falling goats.
  Take a paper and flip him over, David said.

Golden trumpet, yellow Allamanda vine, you are overtaking
this island,
blossoming under
  its shrill kestrel song.
       Tides shattering against volcanic rocks,
         save me.

Dive-bomb

Swarming from ocean-green shadow,
      iridescent turquoise dragonflies gilded copper-silver
—devil's darning needles—
sewing together toes and fingers as we sleep, our eyes shuttered
    "wool-white as sea foam":
  boat people from Burma, Vietnam, Cambodia, Afghanistan—fleeing
violence, human trafficking, repatriation, and "waiting room" refugee
  camps, to go to a Christmas Island—sail
    through circulating gyres of microscopic pelagic plastics
      —polymers, monomers—and chemical sludge from ports, harbors,
  docks, marinas, storm drains, cargo ships, oil-drilling platforms,
fishing vessels: a trash vortex not even visible to divers, much less
    the rest of us. Ocean of Being, we call it. No irony.
      Magic enough to sell sea-salt aerosol hair sprays, MP3 of a
      single wave crashing onshore, beach T-shirts capturing flotsam
from a live-feed of the Pacific. We cast ourselves out. *Full of*
    voids, as *The New York Times* reports, *predominantly lungs,*
    which, when we free dive to 436 feet, collapse
    by more than half: and when we rise,
  unable to absorb oxygen, suffocate ourselves. Atoms forged
in starburst we jump again into the Blue Hole. Sure
  that we'll still be here as the planet cools, volcanoes cease,
    carbon dioxide falls, long before the sun burns down.
We are so sure we bless ourselves in the waters.

Galaxy Filament

Of time evaporating, of my mother's finger
running down my nose during the uncording
ceremony, after she died, the vast sky,
the Milky Way neighborhood,
and me, and David, and the black cat growing tumors,
rain falling, drops left over, puddles gathering,
reflecting the baby birds, black millipedes dropping
off branches, white blossoms floating below cedar,
sunrays bleaching shells, stop signs fading,
a family of wild donkeys milling around
an outdoor basketball court at noon in high heat,
sargassum mats drifting from the horse latitudes
into Drunk Bay, flush with plastic waste and
eel nests, washing onto sandstone rocks,
a lost rubber raft cast ashore with a long towline dragging in the surf,
chickens jump-flapping off trash heaps filled with twisted stair railings
and corrugated roofs blown off by 30 tornados
of two Cat 5 hurricanes, red dust from the Sahara Desert
sifting toward us, nutrients feeding the phytoplankton
but also pathogenic bacteria of the genus *Vibrio,*
iguanas digging nests into the ground and burying their eggs
until hatchlings crack the shells, wait underground
until each emerges, then one after the other, in a line,
scratch their way out. A lone heron soars across the bay.

Of the Wind

whence it arises,
heat of waters, galaxy popping—
ghost of planetary
ringing & spinning:
do I repeat myself, well
so does the moon,
dark surface lit
by ancient crystal highlands
in synchronous rotation
with the earth,
and so the sun,
internal convective whirring a magnetic field.

   Of my mother,
regarding a white orchid
flowering in bilateral symmetry
—petals swirling to violet centers:
I'd like to tell her
of the circular
Aztec temple
uncovered in Mexico City—
coiled like a serpent,
doorway through its nose. No,
I'd like to tell her about
the caper blossom we found,
nocturnal opening

   as pungent as gardenia,
gold-tipped narrow petals
like optic nerve fringe.
And she'd remind us
trees have language—.
Of the day,
one of her last,
quarks spinning, neutrinos

streaming through our bodies. . . .
Of the move
into David's star-shuttered house,
unpacking my fish fossils, pine cones—
and Ana Mendieta art books,

  a silueta of the self
inscribed in mud, sand and
wildflowers. Mother,
you would have clapped.

Ring Finger

To go nameless, the peculiarity:
        a spiny tree—spiked with oval chartreuse apples—
rooted near a brackish salt-pond nursery for birds we can't see or identify
        on a road disappearing into tangled mangroves. Nearby, hooves
scuffle in scrub, wild donkeys, I suppose, on land grazed by cattle, owned
        by people we don't know. Maybe: *manzanilla de la muerte,*
little apple of death—our guidebooks say if you stand under it in rain
        your skin blisters; burn its wood and smoke fogs your eyes.
Caribs soaked arrow-tips in its poison sap. You and I walk around
        intertwining trunks, not knowing where we are, not caring—
but are sure we will arrive home, one hand in the other's,
        content, not sensing harm in the woods, nor in our fingertips,
although we're certain to injure the other, sure to forgive.
        Do you know the other phrase for ring finger? *Nameless one.* Now
rare, but in many languages—German, for instance—believed
        to be a magical digit with a vein running straight to the heart.

Three Views of Darkness

We light up the night
as if it were an unoccupied country
        emptying the sky of stars,
pumping it full of orange haze.
        Call it blind-sight,

this ancient ability to see, using a primal
subcortical subconscious visual system—even
        someone whose lobes are destroyed
can navigate obstacle courses because our border cells
        fire close to a boundary.—

*

Three pairs of men on motorcycles in Kandahar
spray girls' faces with acid, because they go to school—
across eyelids and cheeks; vision goes blurry,
but they return to class.
And in Gaza

a member of the Hamas underground sees
marriage as *jihad*
—producing another generation
that believes in resistance.
If you think *spiral,*

*

consider *Lie* (pronounced *lee*) *group*—
in which symmetries come from continuous
        transformations, some so small.
You and I aren't as fancy
        or dextrous as E8,

the curvy, torus-type object
that's 248-dimensional,
        or at least I don't think we are,
so maybe we should just embrace three: climb
        aboard your old truck, drive toward the North Star.

Landing

And about his touch:
　　　　slightly salty, sun-brown;
pressing down into bedsheets, faint aroma of pool,
　　　　　　　nestling of green palm fronds on window.

And then trying another way.

Tan earlobe, blue-speckled eyes, round sides and feet, the soles.

Relaxing, finally.

Sound from somewhere inside me I'm not familiar with. As if I evaporated
　　　　to reappear. Shorn, stepping outside myself. No,

in the mirror, afterward, recognizing my mother's white hair,
remembering her saying how much she liked mine, when it was long,
　　　　　　　　and then

　　　　grief like a sudden thing;
　　　　　　　　　or so it seemed.

　　　　　　*

Stepping barefoot
　　　　into a tidal bay, slipping into briny waves;
　　　　　　thinking of what lies deeper
　　　　　　than I will go:
basket stars extending arms like nets
　　　　　　　　　to catch small crustaceans.
　　Lava crystalizing into glass
　　　　　　　as it tumbles through Mesopelagic waters.
　　　　　　Consider, from the time of Pliny
　　until the 19th century, no one thought there was life
　　　　at great depths. You say I am melancholy, but how beautiful

80

to think of what lies further out:

if regret is part of this,
                     so be it.

Notes

"And: Still"
Velázquez quote from Jennifer Senior's *New York Times* review of *The Vanishing Velázquez*. Borrowed language from the book by Laura Cumming.

"Contraction"
Quote is from Robert Macfarlane's *Landmarks*.
Borrowed language from Charles Seife's *Zero: The Biography of a Dangerous Idea*.

"Specula"
The passage "Her name was Page . . ." derives from a funeral oration in Ralph Ellison's *Invisible Man* and includes the phrase "born of women to live a while and fall and die" and the sentence "Then you go home and forget it."

"I Am"
This poem is inspired by—and includes lines from—John Clare's "I Am."

"The Last Day We Were All Together"
Borrowings from Noah Gallagher Shannon's "Letter of Recommendation: Arroyos" in *The New York Times*. The sentence beginning "The fullness achieved . . ." is from Shannon's article.

"About a House"
Shirly Hook of the Koas Abenaki Nation, a member of the Vermont Commission for Native American Affairs, as well as Eloise Beil, curator at the Lake Champlain Maritime Museum, consulted about the mention of Abenaki lands.

Line beginning, "*It flows over us . . .*" is composed of re-lineated lines from Robert Frost's "West-Running Brook."

Becky Munsterer Sabky wrote about my mother in her *Valley News* editorial, "Those Strangers Somehow Look Familiar."

Acknowledgments

Much appreciation to the editors at the following literary journals who published these poems, sometimes in earlier versions with different titles:

The Account: "Breaking Wheel," "Physicists Simulate Sending Particles of Light into the Past, Strengthening the Case that Time Travel Is Possible"

American Journal of Poetry: "Age"

American Poetry Review: "Galaxy Filament," "My Unborn Child Says to Me"

At Length: "About a House"

The Cortland Review: "I Am," "Vocal Balance," "XX"

Diode Poetry Journal: "The Last Day We Were All Together"

Great River Review: "Habituate," "Of Liberty"

The Kenyon Review: "Dive-bomb," "Specula"

Laurel Review: "Else," "OO"

Literary Imagination: "Complicit"

On the Seawall: "And: Still"

Plume: "Black Apples," "Excavations from the Tomb of the Second Pharaoh, 12th Dynasty," "Hook," "Landing," "Parable," "Sidewinder," "Vortex Street"

Poetry Northwest: "Contraction"

Utsunomiya University Journal: "I Am," "Sentence," "XX"

West Branch: "Edge Effect," "Ring Finger"

Thank you to Barrow Street Press for offering this manuscript and my previous one a home. Peter Covino for his visionary direction and belief in my work. Sharon Dolin for her time and attention, close reading, and astute editing.

Thank you to my partner David Baker for his guidance, support, and love.

Thank you to Alexandra Krithades for her boundless patience, generosity, and wisdom.

It makes all the difference in the world.

Page Hill Starzinger's first poetry collection, *Vestigial*, selected by Lynn Emanuel to win the Barrow Street Book Prize, was published in 2013. Her chapbook, *Unshelter*, selected by Mary Jo Bang as winner of the Noemi contest, was published in 2009. Her poems have appeared in *American Poetry Review, Kenyon Review, Fence, West Branch, Pleiades, Volt,* and others. Starzinger was Copy Director at Aveda for almost twenty years, and co-authored *A Bouquet from the Met* (Abrams, 1998). She lives in New York City.

Photo: Daniel Dorsa

BARROW STREET POETRY

Vortex Street
Page Hill Starzinger (2020)

Exorcism Lessons in the Heartland
Cara Dees (2019)

American Selfie
Curtis Bauer (2019)

Hold Sway
Sally Ball (2019)

Green Target
Tina Barr (2018)

Adorable Airport
Jacqueline Lyons (2018)

Luminous Debris: New & Selected Legerdemain
Timothy Liu (2018)

We Walk into the Sea: New and Selected Poems
Claudia Keelan (2018)

Whiskey, X-ray, Yankee
Dara-Lyn Shrager (2018)

For the Fire from the Straw
Heidi Lynn Nilsson (2017)

Alma Almanac
Sarah Ann Winn (2017)

A Dangling House
Maeve Kinkead (2017)